It's Easy To Play
Country 'n' Western.

Wise Publications
London/New York/Sydney

Unauthorised reproduction of any part of this publication by any means including photocopying is an infringement of copyright.

Exclusive Distributors:
Music Sales Limited
8/9 Frith Street, London W1V 5TZ, England
Music Sales Pty. Limited
120 Rothschild Avenue, Rosebery, NSW 2018, Australia

This book © Copyright 1977 by
Wise Publications
UK ISBN 0.86001.360.X
UK Order No. AM 19530

Music Sales complete catalogue lists thousands
of titles and is free from your local music
book shop, or direct from Music Sales Limited.
Please send a cheque or Postal Order for £1.50 for postage to
Music Sales Limited, 8/9 Frith Street, London W1V 5TZ.

Printed in England by
Caligraving Limited Thetford Norfolk

Love Hurts

Words & Music by Boudleaux Bryant

Em   G7   C

pain.   Love   is   like   a   cloud,   holds   a   lot   of

D7   G   C

rain;   love   hurts, _____   love

G   D7   G

hurts. _____   I'm   young   I

Em   C   D7

know,   but   e -   ven   so   I ___ know   a

G   Em   C

thing   or   two   I've   learned   from

Forty Shades of Green

Words and Music by Johnny Cash

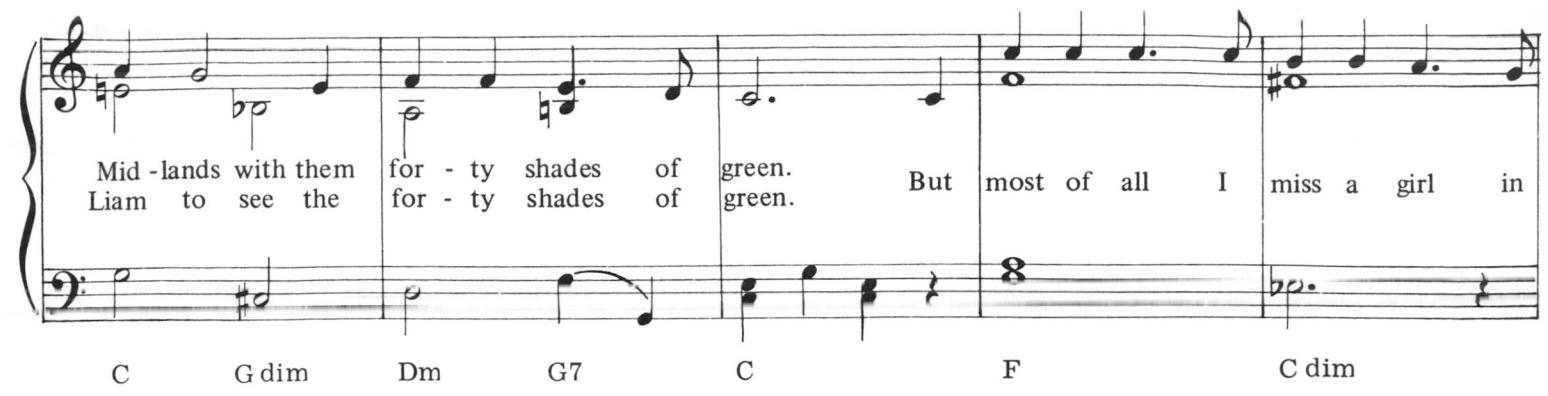

Mid-lands with them for-ty shades of green.　But most of all I miss a girl in
Liam to see the for-ty shades of green.

C　G dim　D m　G7　C　F　C dim

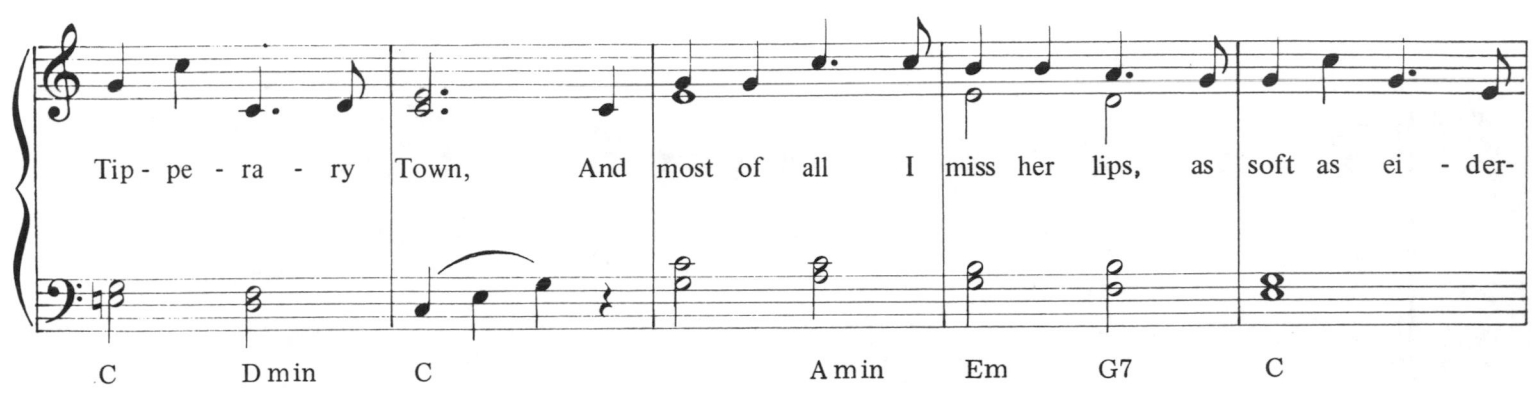

Tip-pe-ra-ry Town,　And most of all I miss her lips, as soft as ei-der-

C　D min　C　A min　Em　G7　C

-down,——　A-gain I want to see and do the things we've done and seen,　Where the

D m7　G　C　F

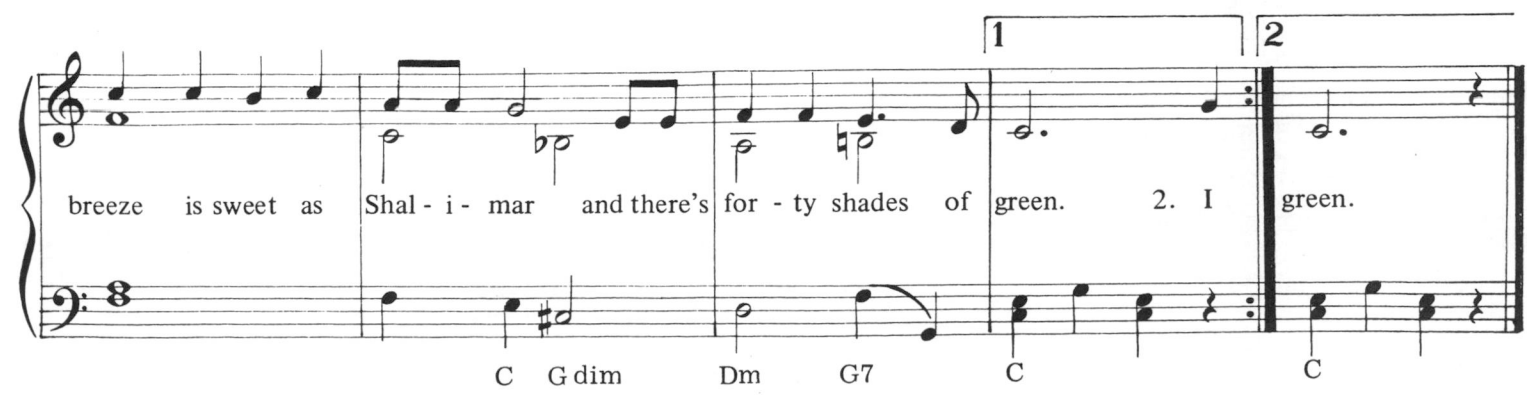

breeze is sweet as Shal-i-mar and there's for-ty shades of green.　2. I　green.

C　G dim　D m　G7　C　C

Green Green Grass Of Home

Words and Music by Curly Putman

good　　to touch　the　green, green, grass　of home.　　　　　　　　　　Yes,　they'll
good　　to touch　the　green, green, grass　of home.　　　　　　　　　　Yes,　they'll

Bb　　　　　　F7　　Cm7 F7　Bb　　　Cm　　Bb

CHORUS

all　　come　to　meet　me,　arms ___ reach - ing,　smil - ing sweet - ly,　it's
all　　come　to　see　me　in　the

(Bb)　　　Bb7　　　　　　Eb

good　　to touch the green, green, grass　of home.　　　　　　　2. The　shade　of that

Bb　　　　　　F7　　Cm7 F7　Bb　　　F7　　　　Eb

rall. . . . . . .

old　oak　tree　as they　lay me 'neath the　green, green grass of　home. ___

Dm Cm　　Bb　　　　　F7　　　　　Eb Dm Cm　Bb

Verse 3. (spoken)　Then I awake and look around me
　　　　　　　　　　at four grey walls that surround me,
　　　　　　　　　　And I realize that I was only dreaming,
　　　　　　　　　　For there's a guard and there's a sad old padre
　　　　　　　　　　—arm in arm we'll walk at daybreak
　　　　　　　　　　Again I'll touch the green, green grass of home.
　　　　　　　　　　　　　　　　　　　　(to Chorus)

Jolene

Words and Music by Dolly Parton

Sixteen Tons

Words and Music by Merle Travis

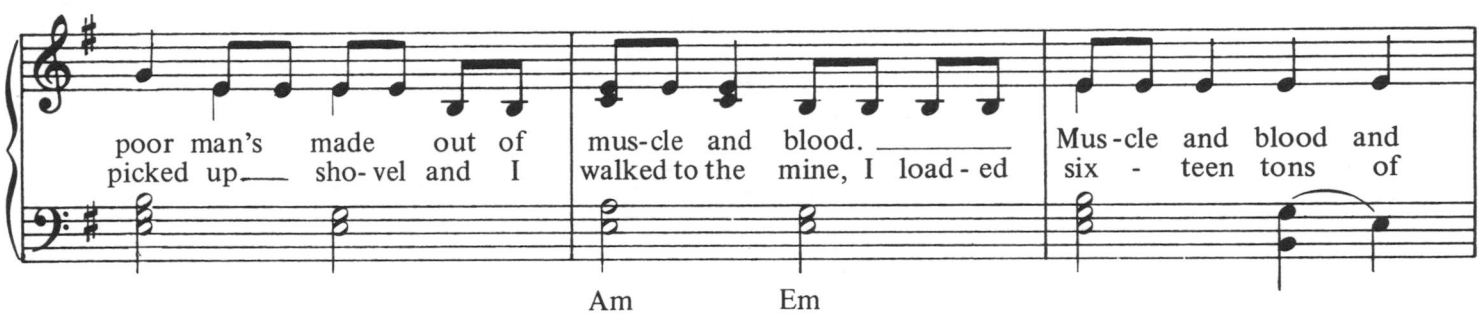

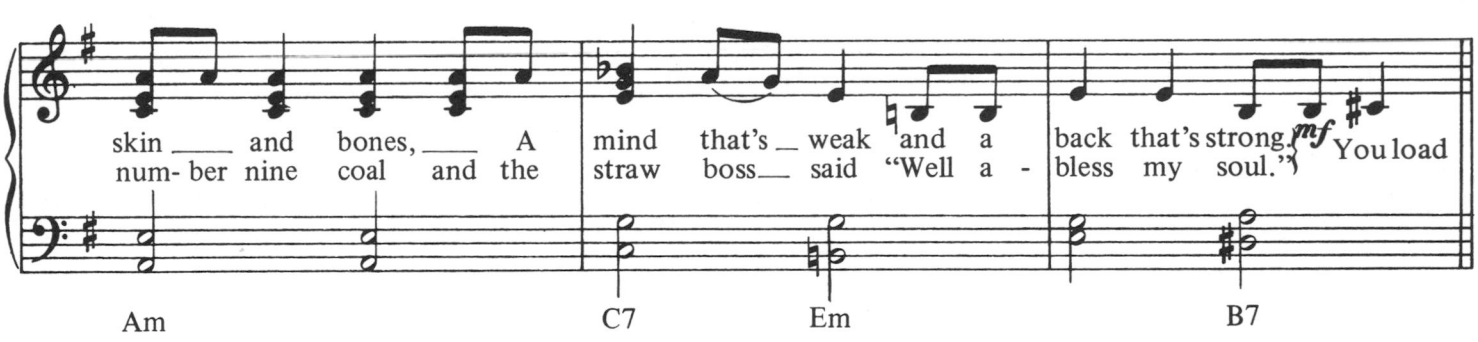

high - toned____ wo - man make me walk the line. *mf* You load
right one don't - a get you, then the left one will. ⎬

C7   Em   B7

six - teen tons what do you get?____ An - oth - er day old - er and

Em   C   Em

deep - er in debt.____ Say bro - ther, don't you call me 'cause I can't go.____ I

Em   C   Am

owe__ my soul to the com - pa - ny store.____ *f*

Em   Am Em Am Em No chord

ritard.   *a tempo* 4. If you *f*   *ritard.*   *sf*
              mp

                            Em No chord   Em

17

Tennessee Waltz

Words and Music by Redd Stewart and Pee Wee King

Moderato

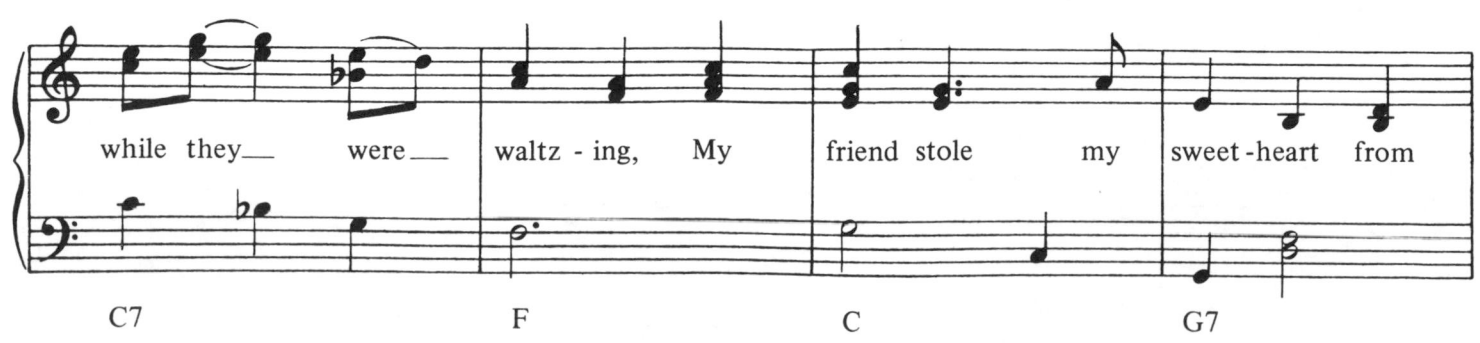

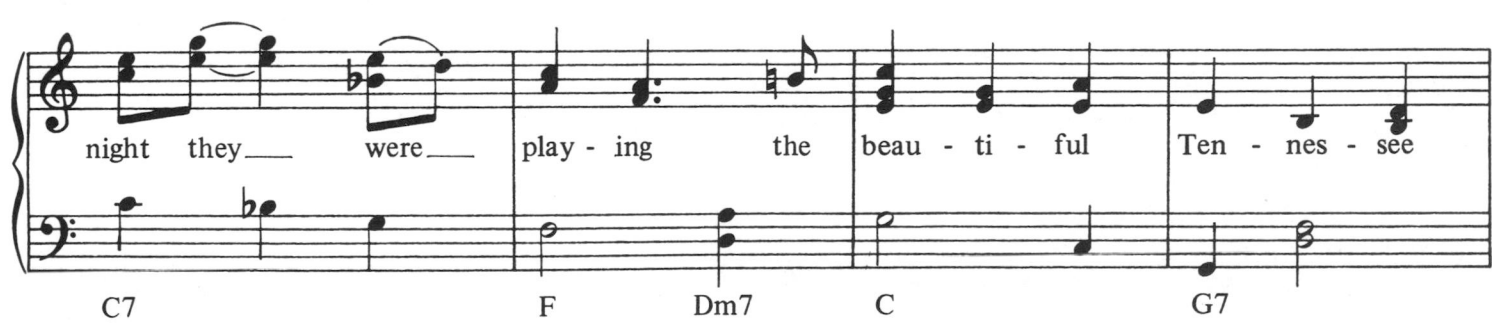

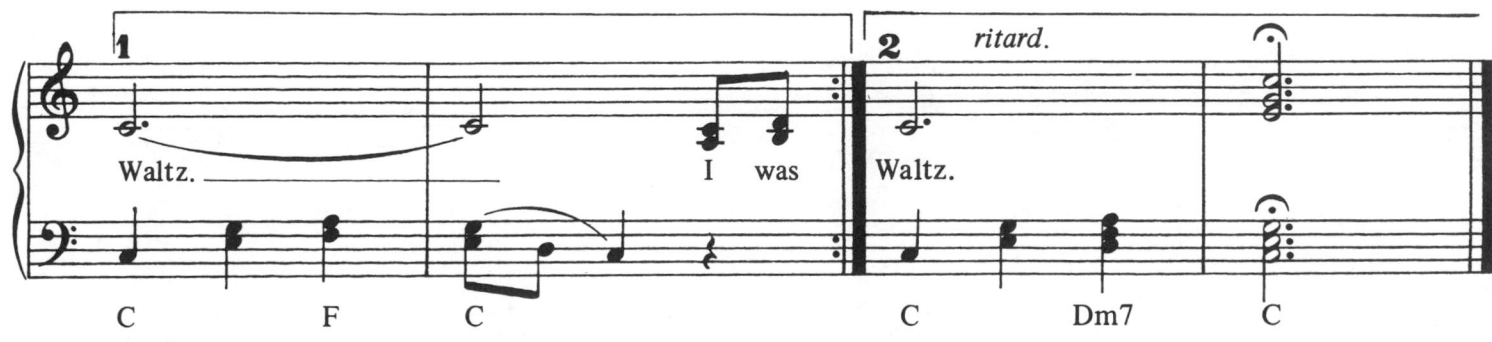

That Old Time Feeling

Words and Music by Baker Knight

I Love You Because

Words and Music by Leon Payne

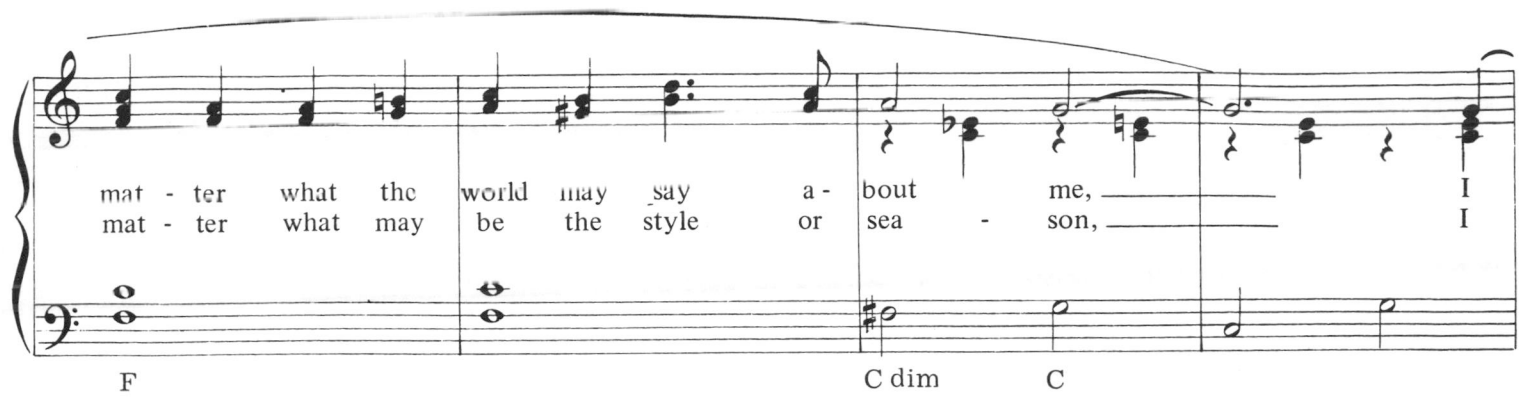

mat - ter what the world may say a - bout me, _____ I
mat - ter what may be the style or sea - son, _____ I

F   C dim   C

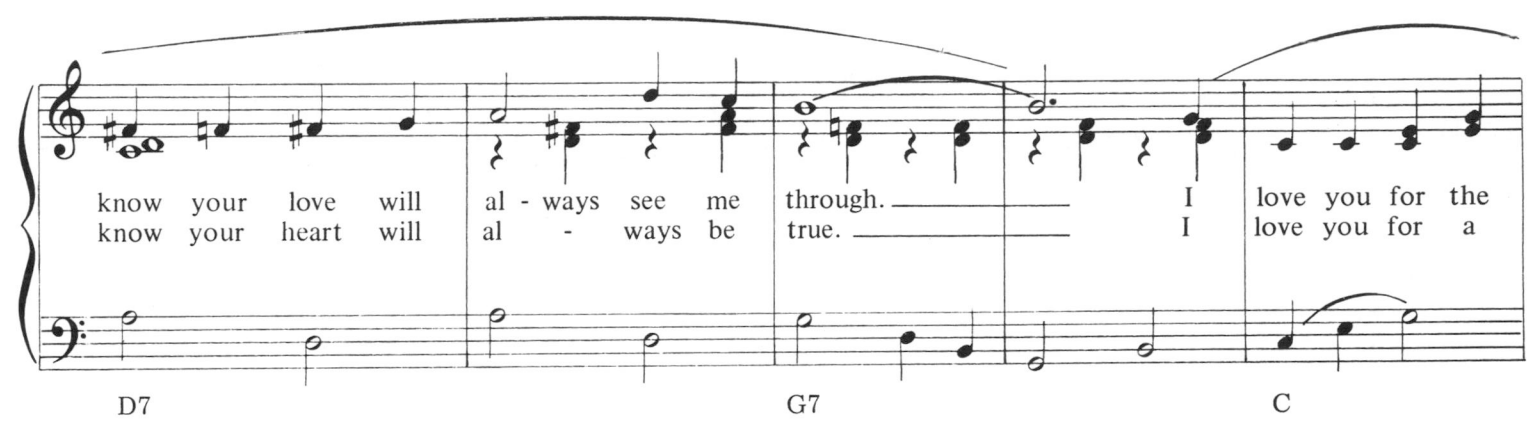

know your love will al - ways see me through. _____ I love you for the
know your heart will al - ways be true. _____ I love you for a

D7   G7   C

way you nev - er doubt me, _____ But most of all I
hun - dred thou - sand rea - sons, _____ But most of all I

C7   F   C

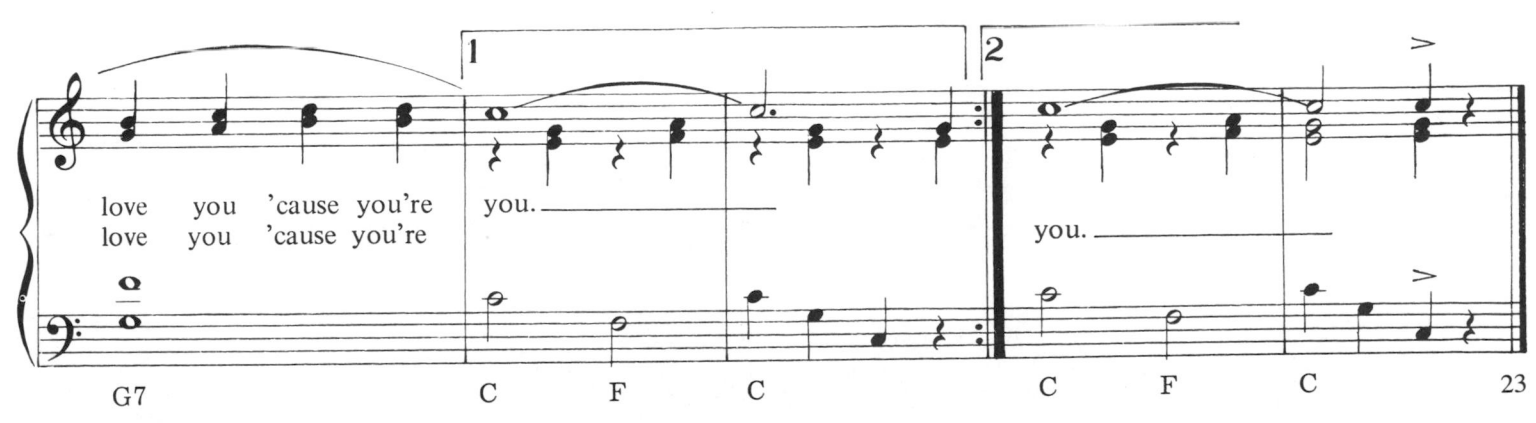

love you 'cause you're you. _____
love you 'cause you're you. _____

G7   C   F   C   C   F   C

Am I That Easy To Forget?

Words and Music by Carl Belew, W.S. Stevenson

But I don't want no one but you. How could you leave with-out re-

gret? Am I that ea-sy to for-get? Be-fore you leave, be

sure you find you want her love much more than mine, 'Cause I'll just say we've
his

ne-ver met, If I'm that ea-sy to for-get.

They say you've found some-bo-dy get.

Eb7   Ab   Eb   Bb7   Eb   Ab   Eb   Eb7   Ab   Eb   Db   Eb7   Ab   Bb   Bb7   Eb   Ab   Eb   Eb   Ab   Eb

25

I'm Going To Be A Country Girl Again

Words and Music by Buffy Sainte-Marie

There Goes My Everything

Words and Music by Dallas Frazier

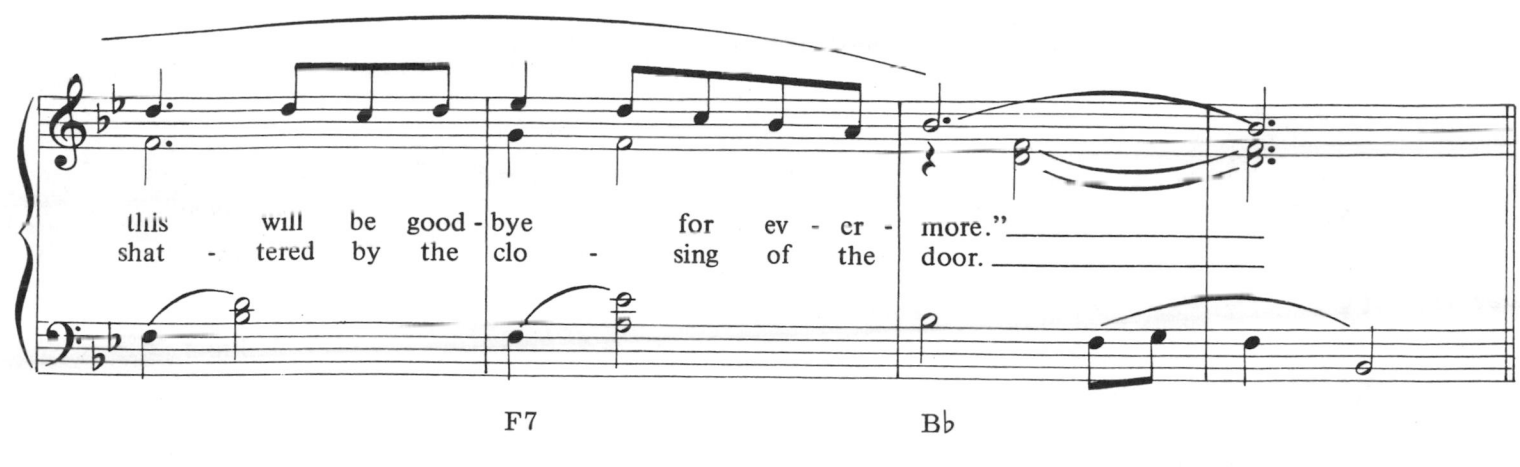

this will be good - bye   for ev - er - more." _____
shat - tered by the clo - sing of the door. _____

F7   Bb

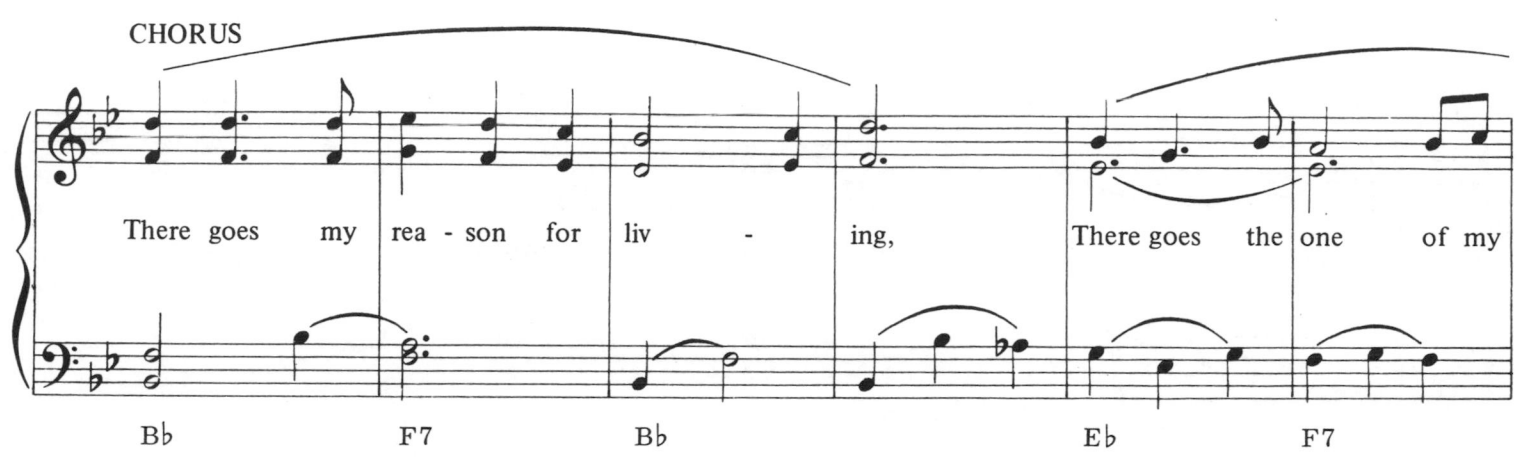

CHORUS

There goes my rea - son for liv - ing,   There goes the one of my

Bb   F7   Bb   Eb   F7

dreams. _____   There goes my on - ly pos - ses - sion,

Bb   F7   Bb   Bb7   Eb

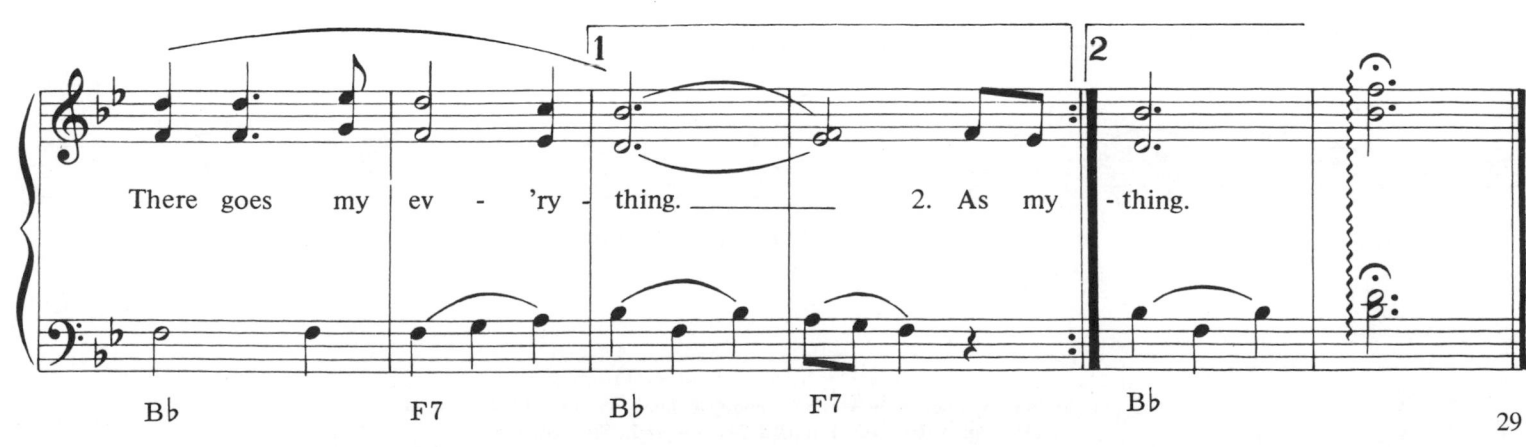

1.
There goes my ev - 'ry - thing. _____

2.
2. As my - thing.

Bb   F7   Bb   F7   Bb

From A Jack To A King

Words and Music by Ned Miller

hand just right to make me king of your heart. For just a

Cm7   F   F7   B♭   E♭   B♭   Fm7   B♭7

lit-tle while, I thought that I might lose the game, Then just in

E♭   E♭dim   B♭   D

time, I saw the twin-kle in your eye. From a Jack to a King,

Gm   Gm7   C7   F   Cm7   F7   B♭

___ from lone-li-ness to a wed-ding ring, I played a ace and I won a queen, ___

B♭dim   Cm   F   F7   Cm7

___ you made me king of your heart. From a Jack to a heart.

F   F7   B♭ E♭ B♭   F7   B♭ E♭   B♭

31

Ruby, Don't Take Your Love To Town

Words and Music by Mel Tillis

To Coda ⊕

town. _____ For it was-n't me that start-ed that old cra-zy A-sia war, _____

F   Gm   B♭   F

____ But I was proud to go and do my pat-ri-ot-ic chores. _____ Oh,

Gm   B♭   C7

I know, Ru-by, that I'm not the man I used to be, _____ but Ru -

B♭   C7   F

D. S. al Coda

-by, _____ I still need your com-pa-ny. _____ 2. It's
3. She's

B♭   C7   F

⊕ CODA

____ For God's sake turn a-round, don't take your love to town. _____

F   B♭   F   B♭   C   F   33

King Of The Road

Words and Music by Roger Miller

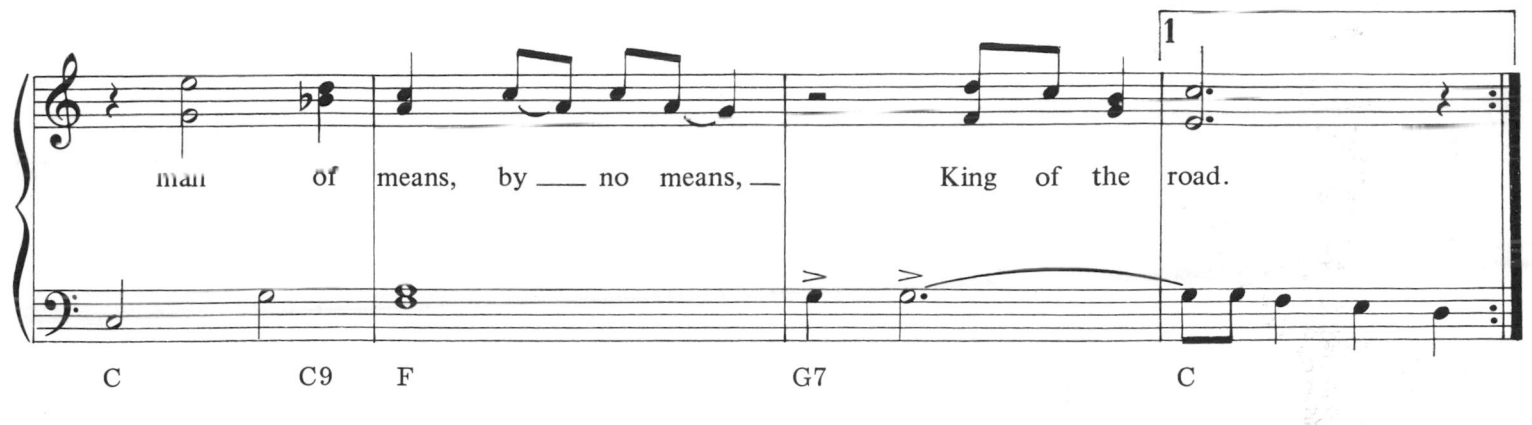

man of means, by ____ no means, ____ King of the road.

C C9 F G7 C

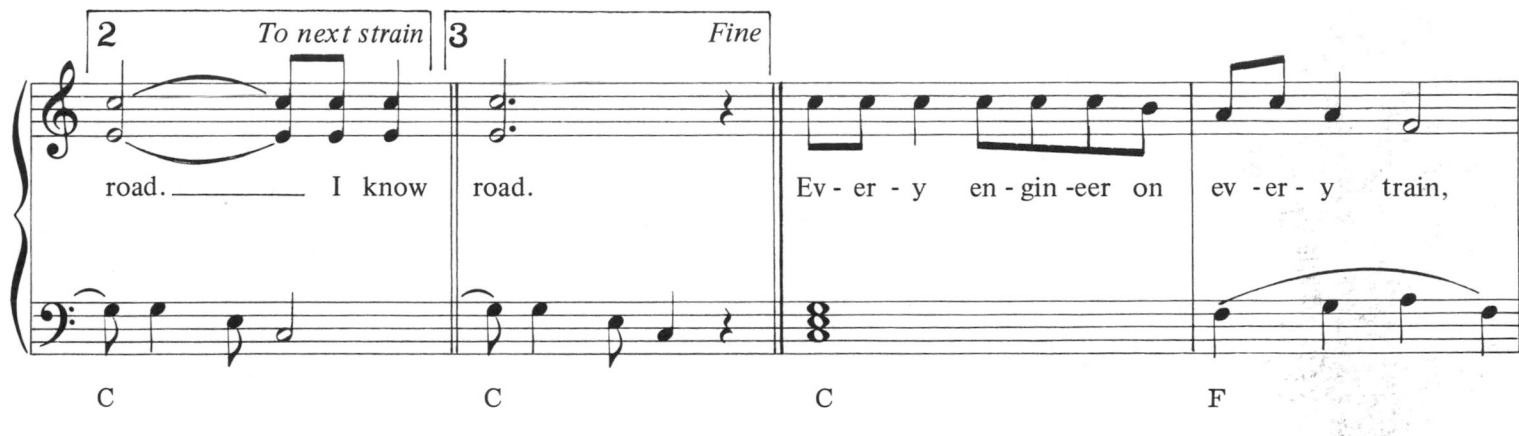

To next strain **Fine**

road. _____ I know road. Ev - er - y en - gin -eer on ev - er - y train,

C C C F

All of the child -ren, and all of their names. And ev - er - y hand - out in

G7 C

D.S. al fine

ev - er - y town and ev' - ry lock that ain't locked when no - one's a - round, I sing

F G G7

35

Blue Bayou

Words & Music by Roy Orbison & Joe Melson

Moderately

I feel so bad ___ I got a wor - ried mind;

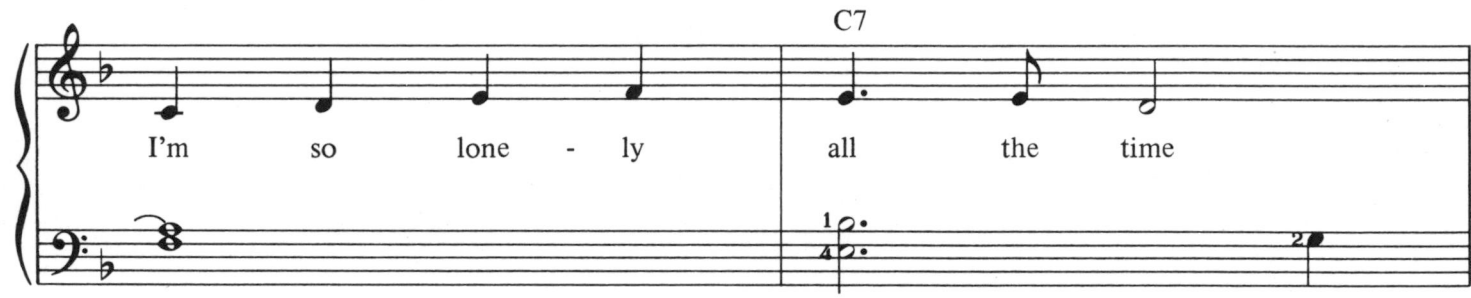

I'm so lone - ly all the time

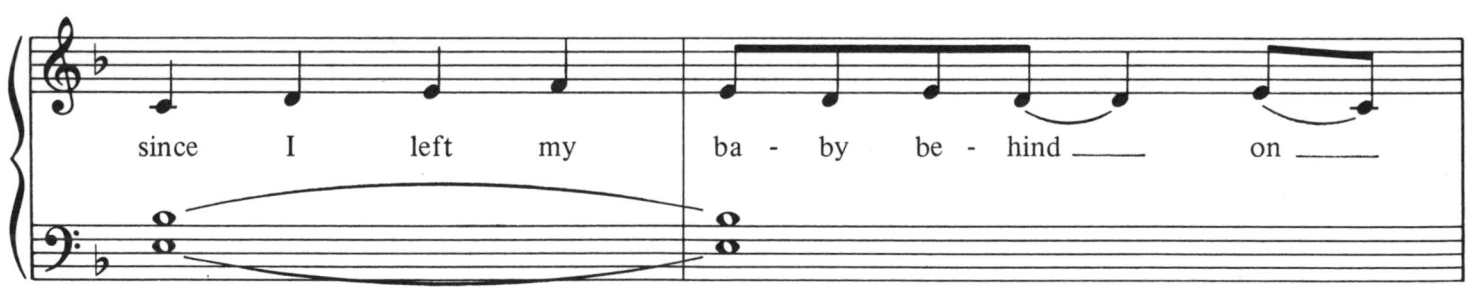

since I left my ba - by be - hind ___ on ___

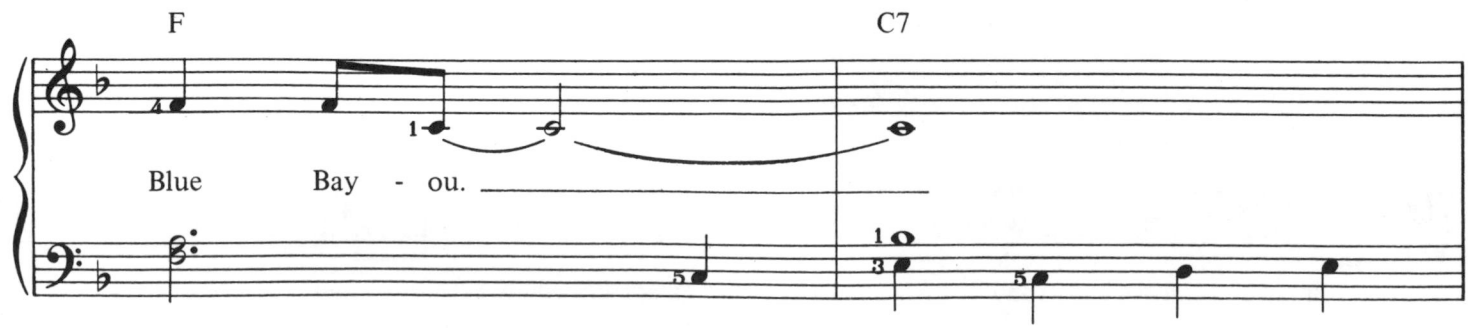

Blue Bay - ou. ___

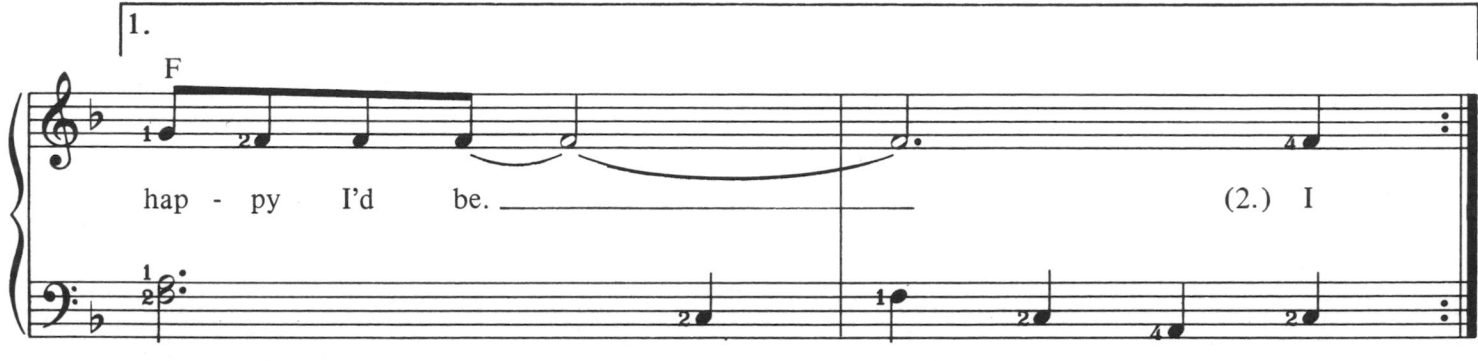

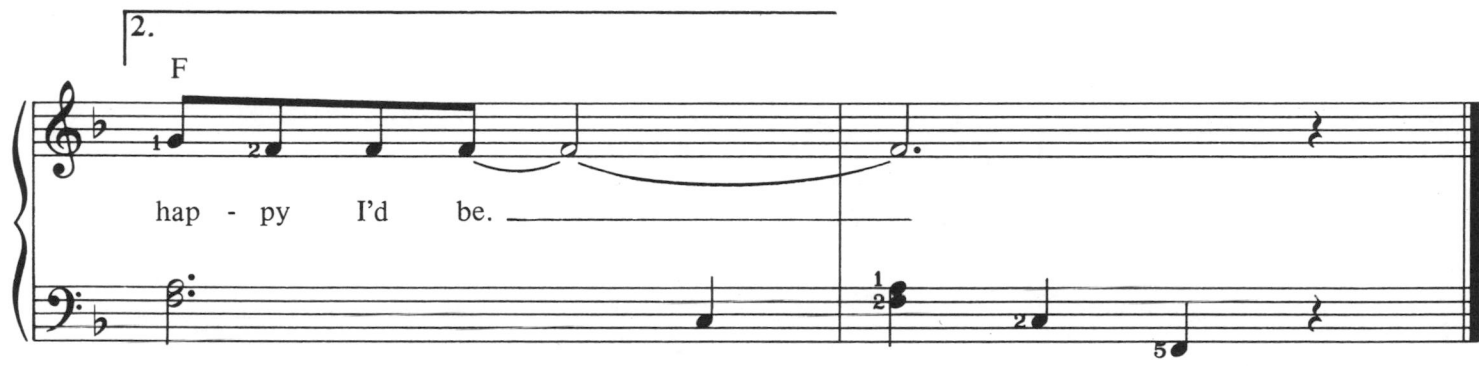

VERSE 2:
I feel so bad, I got a worried mind,
I'm so lonely all the time
Since I left my baby behind on Blue Bayou.
Saving nickles, saving dimes, working 'till the sun don't shine,
Looking forward to happier times on Blue Bayou.

CHORUS 2:
I'm going back someday, gonna stay on Blue Bayou;
Where my folks I'll find, all the time on Blue Bayou.
With that girl of mine by my side
Till the moon in the evening dies,
Oh, some sweet day, gonna take away this hurtin' inside.

For The Good Times

Words and Music by Kris Kristofferson

bri-dges that we're burn-ing.
sad-ness when you leave me. _____ Lay your head _____ up-on my

Gm7   C7   F

pil-low, _____ Hold your warm _____ and ten-der bo-dy close to mine. _____

C7   F

_____ Hear the whis-per of the rain-drops blow-ing soft a-gainst the

B

win-dow and make be-lieve you love me _____ one more time

Gm7   C7

_____ for the good times. _____ I'll get a-   times.

F   F

41

Cryin' Time

Words and music by Buck Owens

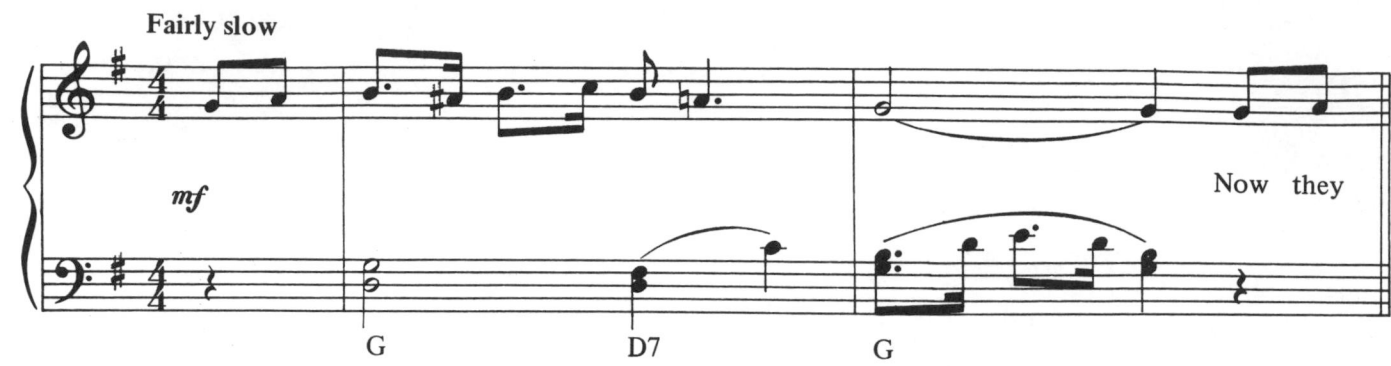

leave me,___ I can see that far a-way look___ in your eyes; I can

tell ___ by the way you___ hold me dar-lin', That it won't be long be-fore it's___ cry-in'

Fine

time._____ Now you said that you've some-one___ you love bet-ter, ___ That's the

way it's hap-pened ev'-ry time be-fore, And as sure ___ as the sun comes up to-

D.S. al Fine

mor-row;___ Cry-in' time will start when you walk___ out the door. Oh, it's

Lucille

Words and Music by Roger Bowling and Hal Bynum

In a bar in To - le - do, a - cross from the de - pot, on a
mir - ror, I saw him and I close - ly watched him, I

bar stool she took off her ring. I thought I'd get clo-
thought how he looked out of place. He came to the wo-

ser, so I walked on ov - er, I sat down and asked her her name
man who sat there be - side me, he had a strange look on his face.

When the drinks fin - 'ly hit her, she said "I'm no
The big hands were cal - loused, he looked like a

quit-ter, but I fin-'lly quit liv-ing on dreams._____ I'm
moun-tain, for a min-ute I thought I was dead._____ But

F7   Bb Bbdim Bb7   Eb

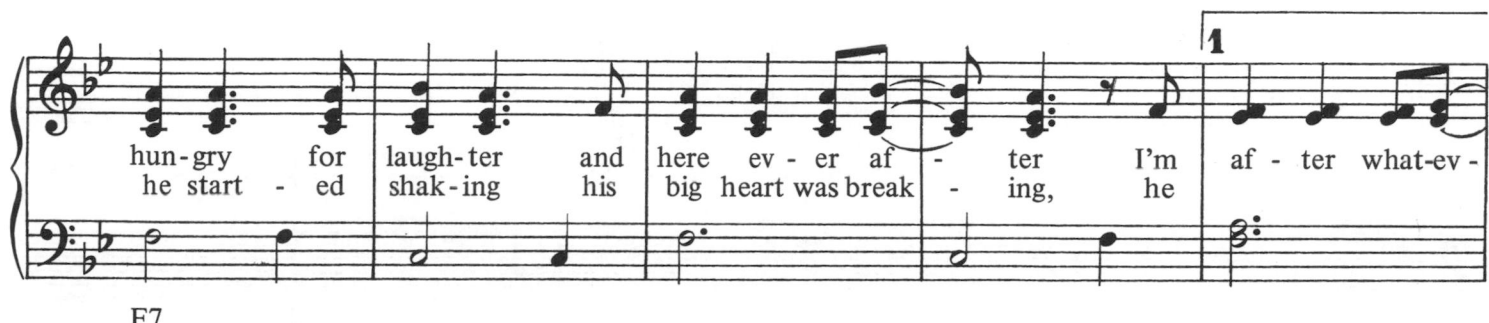

hun-gry for laugh-ter and here ev-er af - ter, I'm
he start - ed shak-ing his big heart was break - ing, he

F7

___ er the oth-er life brings."_____ In the
turned to the

Bb   F7

wo-man and said:_____ You picked a fine time to leave___ me, Lu-

Bb

cille._____ With four hun-gry chil - dren and a crop in the

Eb   Fb Eb   Bb

field. _____ I've had some bad times, lived through some

Eb

sad times, but this time your hurt-in' won't heal. _____ You picked a

Bb

fine time to leave me, Lu - cille. _____

F7   Bb   C

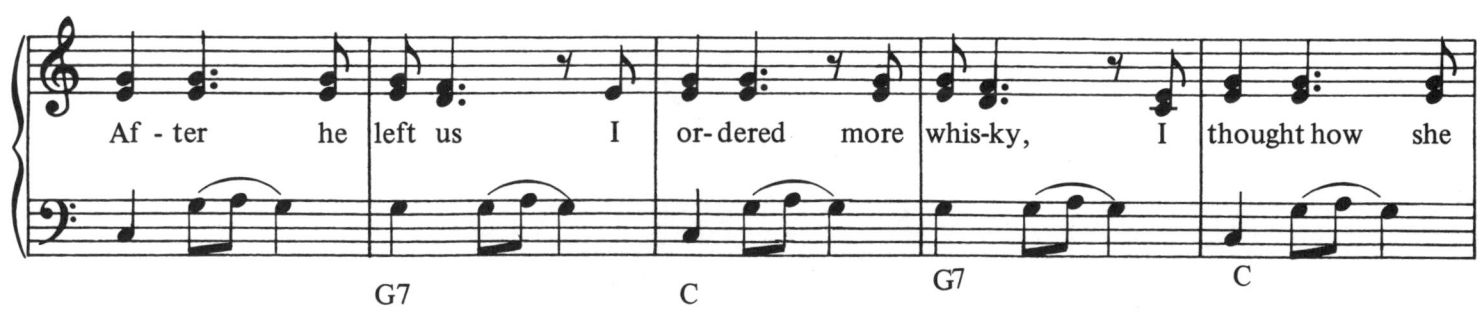

Af - ter he left us I or-dered more whis-ky, I thought how she

G7   C   G7   C

made him look small. _____ From the lights of the bar - room to a

G7 C G7   Dm

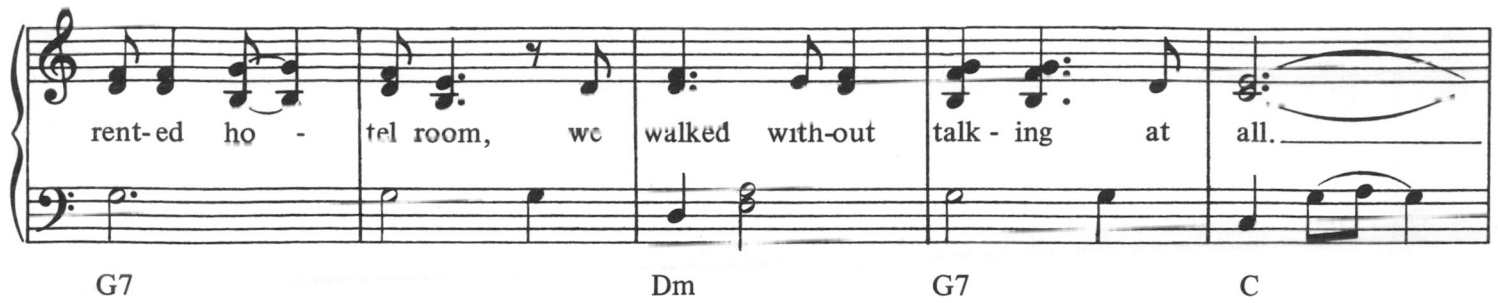

G7   Dm   G7   C

rent-ed ho - tel room, we walked with-out talk - ing at all. ____

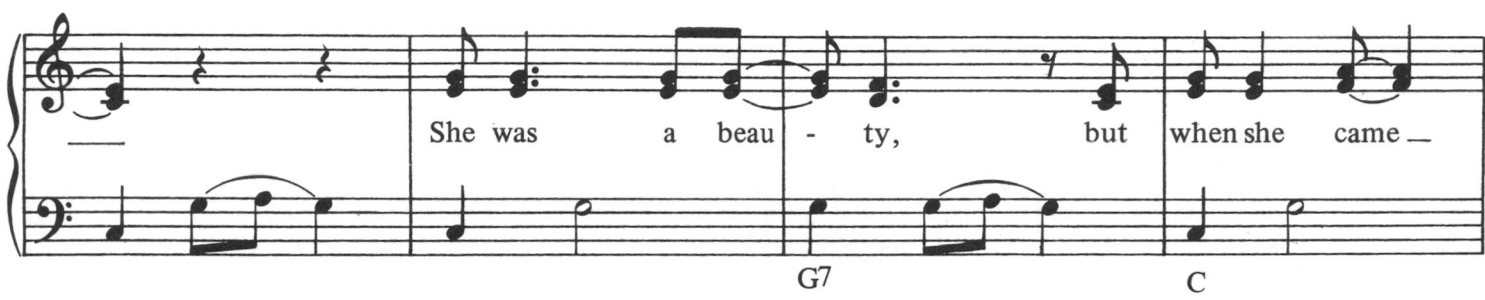

G7   C

____ She was a beau - ty, but when she came ____

G7   C7   F

to me, she must - 've thought I'd lost my mind. ____

G7

____ I could - n't hold ____ her 'cause the words that he told ____

C

____ her, kept com-ing back time af - ter time. ____ You picked a

47

fine time to leave ___ me, Lu - cille, ___ with

F

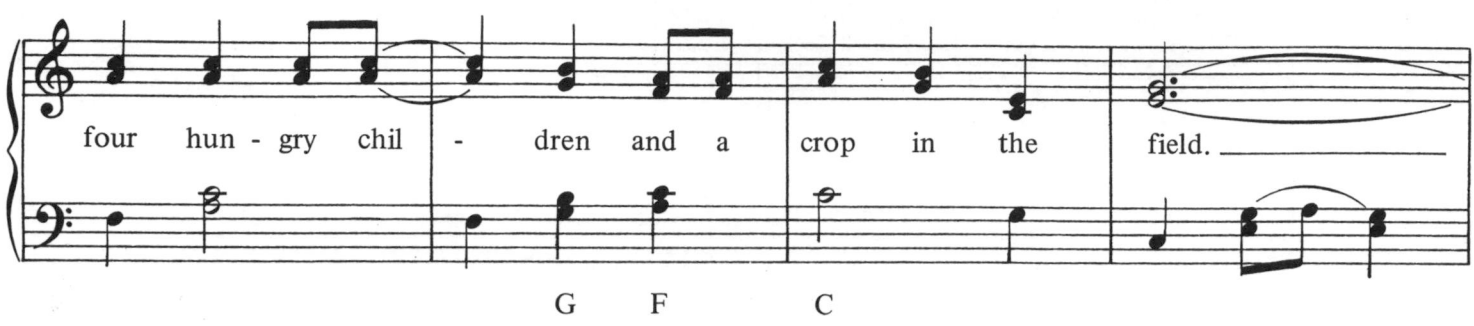

four hun - gry chil - dren and a crop in the field. ___

G   F   C

I've had some bad times, __ lived through some

F

sad times, __ but this time your hurt - in' won't heal. ___

C

Repeat and fade

__ You picked a fine time to leave me, Lu - cille. ___ You picked a

G7   C

09/03 (48519)